M.D. Tophus. The Controversy of the Remorseless and Unempathic Healthcare
          Worker.

Copyright ©. 2023. M.D. Tophus.

Hilphma Publications 2023. www.hilphmapublication.com

First Edition.

Germany.

The author has over 25 years of clinical experience in the healthcare field. Is cognisant of both DSM-5-TR (and previous versions) and ICD-11 (and previous versions) disorders and conditions; quality and safety improvement in healthcare; and healthcare education.

Other M.D. Tophus publications available:

"Exercising Quality in Healthcare Service Provision: A Complex Care Workbook for All Healthcare Professionals." Germany: Hilphma Publications: 2022.

"Who is This Colleague?: Dangers of the Healthcare Profession, and beyond. An Interview Guide for Recruitment, Performance Appraisal and Post-Adverse Events."
Germany: Hilphma Publications: 2022.

"Think on your Feet: Those Who Can. For the Consummate Healthcare Professional."
Germany: Hilphma Publications: 2022.

"The Unfortunate Healthcare Treater, The Hapless Healthcare Therapist: Narcissistic and Borderline Personality Disorder clients. The Grit."
Germany: Hilphma Publications: 2022.

"Victims of Crime: Introduction to Forensic Challenges in Healthcare."
Germany: Hilphma Publications: 2022.

"The A to Z of Workplace Bullying: For the Healthcare Professional and Beyond."
Germany: Hilphma Publications: 2022.

"Trauma United, Life Defined. A Healthcare Tool for Professionals Across the Globe."
Germany: Hilphma Publications: 2022.

"Reflective Thinking: the True Healthcare Tool."
Germany: Hilphma Publications: 2022.

"Burnout in Healthcare"
Germany: Hilphma Publications: 2022.

"Reasonable Resilience in Workplaces and Healthcare Work"
Germany: Hilphma Publications: 2022.

"The Psychological Impacts of Labelling and Failure to Diagnose"
Germany: Hilphma Publications: 2022.

CONTENTS

Page

8   Introduction

10   Remorse

14   Empathy

16   Remorselessness

18   Lack of Empathy

24   Callousness

26   Disinhibition

27   Assessment Measures of Personality Disorders with Emphasis on Identification of Remorselessness and Lack of Empathy

37   Patient impacts

40   Questions

46   Abbreviations

49   References

54   Index

The healthcare worker who is typically disliked- to hated- by others, is one who incites and pursues their frightening life philosophy and behavioral traits, relentlessly, regardless of differing opinions, presentations of angst and opposition, and official reprimands.

For they are the ultimate, in their own eyes, as the optimal successor to weaker colleagues. Their apparatus is always governed by their lack of empathy, rejection of the concepts between right and wrong, and ultimately, their remorselessness.

Faced with ethical dilemmas, through to never events, in medical error- within the healthcare environment-, this individual resembles wolverine capacities.

This publication examines the resourcefulness of the remorseless and unempathic healthcare professional, their capabilities of endangering others, the significance of their existence within the healthcare field, assessment processes, and the impacts upon patients and healthcare colleagues, alike.

The M.D. Tophus publication:

"Who is This Colleague?: Dangers of the Healthcare Profession, and beyond. An Interview Guide for Recruitment, Performance Appraisal and Post-Adverse Events."

is an essential supplemental to this current resource. Not only for the recruiters, performance appraisers, or post-adverse event involved personnel, but to each reader of this current publication.

REMORSE

Remorse is understood as:

"prolonged and insistent self-reproach and mental anguish for past wrongs and especially for those whose consequences cannot be remedied" (1).

It also encompasses: "a feeling of being sorry for doing something bad or wrong in the past: a feeling of guilt" (2)

and: a "strong sense of guilt and regret for a past action" (3).

Shame:

is usually an emotional feeling elicited because others are aware of guilt-based conduct.

-Feelings of **guilt** relate to negative behavioral reaction or contemplation upon a particular situation, action etc, often culminating in **remorse plus regret.**

-The difference between **regret and remorse** requires emphasis.

Regret involves many negative emotions.

Although directly connected to remorse, it differs from remorse by the focus upon affects to self and the avoidance of future punishment.

<u>**Healthcare focus:**</u>

-Shame,

-guilt,

-sadness,

-rumination,

can be some of the effects upon those involved in the negative action.

egs of physiological symptomatology, are:

-insomnia,

-nightmares,

-physical and emotional exhaustion.

<u>**Anticipated regret:**</u>

-preventative inaction, or preventative action/regret avoidance, respectively, creates higher risk circumstances or perceivably lower ones.

In the case of healthcare work, it may be experienced when faced with:

-an imminent task (similar to one which went awry in the past),

-a high risk based duty, or

-one which triggers memories of a critical incident/ medical error.

Open disclosure in healthcare environments:

-Open disclosure, and apologies, following an adverse healthcare event highlight the importance of expressions of remorse.

Please note, that this explanation of 'open disclosure' excludes:

-'dotting the i's and crossing the t's,

-mandatory obligation,

-that one has officially said 'sorry', or

-because management/human resources said so'

grounds for open disclosure.

The open disclosure process commonly involves:

-the use of 'sorry' as communication of regret about the healthcare incident,

-factual description of what occurred,

-prevention of recurrence and any plans to manage the incident,

-patient feedback.

<u>**Open disclosure, as desirable and appropriate:**</u>

> Lazare (4) wrote extensively on open disclosure:
>
> "The third part of an apology is the expression of remorse, shame, forbearance, and humility.....Lack of remorse, shamelessness, unwillingness to address the future, and arrogance will undo most apologies" (4).

Thus, typical <u>sequential stages of guilt</u> (experienced by functional healthcare workers/ those capable of remorse), involve:

> -shock;
>
> -repudiation;
>
> -anger;
>
> -negotiation;
>
> -deep sadness;
>
> -acceptation;
>
> -processing of the guilt.

EMPATHY

Empathy is defined as:

"the action of understanding, being aware of, being
sensitive to, and vicariously experiencing the feelings, thoughts, and experience
of another of either the past or present without having the feelings, thoughts and
experience fully communicated in an objectively explicit manner" (5).

Empathy is also: "the ability to share someone else's feelings or experiences by
imagining what it would be like to be in that person's situation" (6)

and: "understanding a person from his or her frame of reference rather than one's
own, or vicariously experiencing that person's feelings, perceptions, and thoughts"
(7).

**Though there are many different <u>understandings of Empathy</u>, the
following generally applies:**

<u>Affective Empathy:</u>

-also known as Emotional Empathy,

-is the ability to understand and respond in an appropriate way (compassionate
expression) to another individual's emotions.

-Moreover, it is the capacity to <u>feel</u> the other's emotions.

This differs from **Cognitive Empathy**, which is essentially:

-the capacity to understand and _imagine_ the emotions being felt by another, and

-being able to place yourself in another's shoes, so to speak.

REMORSELESSNESS

<u>Unremorseful/Remorseless examples specific to healthcare environments, following a critical incident, include:</u>

-admission/internal disclosure (to colleagues) <u>versus</u> true feelings of remorse

-superiority and refusal of <u>accountability</u>

-clinical <u>decision-making</u> and pack mentality

-phenomenological-physiological-happenstance <u>justifications</u> supplanting regret

-<u>self-focussed regret</u>: impact focus solely on healthcare worker effects (often accompanied by deceit)

-<u>risk-taking</u>: not only <u>not</u> experiencing regret, or guilt, but willingness to immediately (and in the future) undertake the same <u>deleterious</u> action again and again

-unthinking actions resulting in <u>future harm</u>, especially evident in medical error situations synonymous or analagous with previous ones

-<u>callous</u> disregard

-<u>contempt</u> for those expressing remorse, or for those who suffered as a result of the action for which others are expressing remorse

-<u>rationalization and coldness </u>(and insouciance) regarding concept of guilt, remorse

-<u>glibness</u> (also inclusive in lack of empathy category).

From an <u>anti-social personality disorder</u> perspective:

-Lack of anxiety regarding the situation, action, medical event or negative clinical decision-making; and,

-"lack of concern for the feelings, needs, or suffering of others; lack of remorse after hurting or mistreating another" (8).

This explanation also incorporates the <u>lack of empathy</u> within such individuals.

LACK OF EMPATHY

There are many different reasons for <u>exercising lack of empathy</u>.

These include (from the potentially forgivable, to the less forgivable):

<u>Burnout:</u>

"Symptoms are in the realms of depersonalization, emotional exhaustion and feelings of decreased personal accomplishment in work activities" (9).

<u>Feeling overwhelmed:</u>

-perceived inability to take on another's emotions

-similar to elements of burnout

-feeling as if 'head will explode' if one conveys any more empathy, or undertakes further empathic processing.

<u>Trauma triggers:</u>

-self-focus due to reminders of (a) traumatic event/s

-leading to reduced capacity to feel, and express, empathy

-flashbacks, avoidance thereof, and eluding the related trauma triggers, stifles reciprocal emotional presence

-psychological distress overwhelms ability to relate with others

-feeling detached from other

-concentration issues, irritability, and hypervigilance

-vulnerability, and

-feeling that others are aware of one's vulnerable, traumatised state.

Dissociative tendencies:

-emotional processing deficits

-perception difficulties (can alter cognitive and affective empathic processing)

-avoidance of negative emotions in others

-emotional memory dysfunction, which affects historical to present understanding of another's plight

-delay, or minimal, memory recall of another individual's personal and emotional context and state.

<u>**Self-protective avoidance of connection with others:**</u>

-non-trauma related

-coping style which is recurrently practised

-highly pragmatic approach to job role

-anger,

-rejection, and

-intolerance,

is involved.

Also, resentment toward healthcare environment, patients, job duties.

<u>**Emotional dysregulation:**</u>

-emotional reactivity and incapability of listening to others, or similarly- refusal to

-easily frustrated with other individuals

-poor impulse control

-chooses vindictiveness, glibness, refusal to effectively communicate, over relating with another human being

-propensity for conflict, fightability, and sensitivity- purely for one's own needs.

Moreover, though <u>compromization of the capacity for empathy</u> (and sometimes <u>remorse</u>) is prevalent amongst several different personality disorders (including borderline; avoidant; schizotypal; and obsessive-compulsive), the two personality disorders below, are of necessary focus:

<table>
<tr><td>

<u>**Anti-social personality disorder**</u> (sociopathy, and psychopathy, is often used interchangeably):

-cognitive empathy is primarily effected.

<u>**Narcissistic personality disorder:**</u>

-affective empathy in particular is effected.

</td></tr>
</table>

<u>**Anti-social personality disorder:**</u>

As with narcissistic personality disorder, it is entirely possible that there is more than one healthcare professional in a given healthcare environment who fits the description, symptomatology, and diagnostic parameters, of anti-social personality disorder.

A comprehensive description of <u>**Anti-social personality disorder**</u>, involves:

-historical anti-social behaviors occurring from age of 15 years

-diagnosis is made at 18 years and older

-lack of remorse is one key indicator of the disorder

-callous disregard for others (which involves empathy deficits)

-lack of concern, lack of remorse

-lying

-recurrent irresponsibility

-impulsive behaviors

-rejection of social norms

-aggression

-absolute risk-taker

-manipulative.

<u>Narcissistic personality disorder:</u>

-typically diagnosed in adulthood, or at age 18 years and over

-lack of empathy is a primary symptom

-callous

-manipulative

-deceitful

-grandiose

-sense of entitlement

-exploits others on an interpersonal level

-arrogant

-envious

-heavy focus upon fantasising about success and power

-conceptualises self as 'special' and can only be appreciated by 'special others'

-penultimate attention-seeker.

Callousness is defined, diagnostically, as:

"Lack of concern for the feelings or problems of others; lack of guilt or remorse about the negative or harmful effects of one's actions on others" (10).

-It is considered part of anti-social personality disorder, and is synonymous with 'malignant narcissism'

-Callousness is part of Antagonism.

In **Narcissistic personality disorder**:

-grandiosity, and

-attention seeking

predominates.

-(also part of Antagonism).

Malignant narcissism also has antagonism traits of:

-manipulativeness, and

-deceitfulness.

<u>Anti-social personality disorder</u>:

as part of Antagonism includes:

-manipulativeness,

-deceitfulness,

-hostility,

- and, as with <u>psychopathy</u>: high levels of attention-seeking.

DISINHIBITION

Disinhibition is diagnostically defined as:

> "Orientation toward immediate gratification, leading to impulsive behavior driven by current thoughts, feelings, and external stimuli, without regard for past learning or consideration of future consequences" (10).

Disinhibition encompasses:

-irresponsibility,

-impulsivity,

-distractibility,

-risk taking, and

-rigid perfectionism.

-Risk taking,

-impulsivity, and

-irresponsibility

(all effectively part of disinhibition) is considered part of anti-social personality disorder.

ASSESSMENT MEASURES of PERSONALITY DISORDERS
with Emphasis on Identification of
REMORSELESSNESS and LACK of EMPATHY

Assessment of empathy:

Multi-Faceted Empathy Test (MET) english version:

-computerized test;

-40 pictures (20 positive, 20 negative);

-assesses cognitive and emotional empathy
(11).

the Multi-Dimensional Emotional Empathy Scale (MDEES):

-30 items;

-assesses the capacity to comprehend and recognize emotions experienced by
other individuals;

-includes: suffering, positive sharing, responsive crying, emotional
attention, feel for others, and emotional contagion
(12).

Movie for the Assessment of Social Cognition (MASC):

-15 minute movie;

-followed by questions;

-measures perceptions of feelings, thoughts, and intentions (13).

the Interpersonal Reactivity Index (IRI):

-28 items

-measures dispositional empathy;

-four 7 item subscales;

-includes empathic concern, and perspective taking; fantasy; personal distress (14).

the Empathy Quotient (EQ):

-60 items;

-shorter version- 40 items;

-measures cognitive and affective empathy (15).

Empathy Construct Rating Scale (ECRS):

-84 items;

-assessment for nurses and nursing students, and other healthcare professionals;

-self-scored;

-measures empathy on the whole in client and/or patient settings
(16).

Jefferson Scale of Physician Empathy (JSE):

-20 items;

-assesses areas of empathy of physicians in healthcare environments
involving direct contact with patients.

-Jefferson Scale of Empathy also measures empathy in all healthcare professionals
and medical students (S-version) and health professional student.

(HPstudent version):

-measures empathy, compassion, trust, sympathy, tolerance, personal growth,
communication, self-protection, humour and clinical neutrality
(17).

<u>**Therapist Empathy Scale (TES):**</u>

-9 items;

-observation based;

-assesses cognitive, affective, attitudinal, and attunement elements of therapist empathy.

-Also: concern, expressiveness, resonate or capture client feelings, warmth, attuned to client's inner world, understanding cognitive framework, understanding feelings/inner experience, acceptance of feelings/inner experiences, and responsiveness
(18).

<u>**Questionnaire of Cognitive and Affective Empathy (QCAE):**</u>

-15 minutes administration; 31 items;

-assesses perspective taking; emotion contagion; online simulation; peripheral responsivity; proximal responsivity
(19).

<u>Emotional Empathic Tendency Scale (EETS):</u>

-33 items;

-emotional contagion; feelings of others; emotional responsiveness; positive and negative emotional experiences; sympathy; willingness of contact; (20).

<u>For patients:</u>

<u>Decision Regret Scale (DRS):</u>

-patient focus/response, as a form of feedback regarding healthcare decision making:

-patient response based;

- measures "distress or remorse after a (health care) decision" (21).

<u>Consultation and Relational Empathy (CARE) measure:</u>

-10 items;

-assesses quality of care and patient empathy;

-patient use;

-examines overall empathy with focus upon patient-centered approaches in treatment in a variety of settings, including amongst GPs (22).

<u>**Specific to Narcissism, including remorselessness and lack of empathy:**</u>

<u>**Five Factor Narcissism Inventory (FFNI):**</u>

-15 subscales;

-measures narcissistic traits, including grandiose and vulnerable narcissism;

-domains: neuroticism, extraversion, openness, antagonism, and conscientiousness
(23).

<u>**Narcissistic Personality Inventory (NPI):**</u>

-NPI-40: 40 paired items;

-also the NPI-15; NPI-9; NPI-13; and NPI-8;

-non-diagnostic;

-measures narcissistic personality traits; normal and subclinical narcissism levels
(24).

Pathological Narcissism Inventory (PNI)

-52 items;

-measures narcissistic grandiosity and narcissistic vulnerability;

-7 domains (entitlement rage, exploitativeness, grandiose fantasy, self-sacrificing self-enhancement, contingent self-esteem, hiding the self, and devaluing) (25).

In anti-social personality disorder, sociopathy, psychopathy- including remorselessness and lack of empathy:

Hare's Psychopathy Checklist Revised (PCL-R); and PCL-SV:

PCL-R:

-20 items;

-measures emotional detachment and anti-social behavior (26).

PCL-SV: Psychopathy Checklist- Screening Version; shorter version of the PCL-R;

-12 items;

-screens for the possible existence of psychopathy (anti-social personality) and severity of symptoms;

-measures arrogance and deceitfulness; affective deficiency; impulsive and irresponsible behaviors; and a history (in adolescence and adulthood) of criminal offending;

-though also commonly used in a variety of non-forensic contexts
(27).

Psychopathic Personality Inventory Revised (PPI-R):

-154 items;

-anti-social behaviors are not required to be declared by the respondent, the measurement assesses for psychopathy (anti-social personality features, and more);

-clinical features regardless (global psychopathy and traits of psychopathy); fearless dominance; self-centered impulsivity
(28).

<u>**Comprehensive Assessment of Psychopathic Personality (CAPP):**</u>

-full coverage of psychopathy;

-can be used in multiple settings;

-measures severity and longevity of symptoms;

-involves a series of scales;

-eg CAPP SRS: CAPP Symptom Rating Scale (observation based); CAPP SRS- CI
CAPP Semi structured interview- Clinical Interview
(29).

<u>**the Anti-Social Personality Questionnaire (APQ):**</u>

-17 items;

-measures interpersonal and intrapersonal antisocial dispositions; self-control,
self-esteem, avoidance, paranoid suspicion, resentment, aggression, deviance and
extraversion
(30).

<u>**For both npd and anti-social personality disorder (empathy and remorse):**</u>

<u>**the Dirty Dozen test :**</u>

-12 items;

-shortened version of the Dark Triad Dirty Dozen (DTDD); measures psychopathy; narcissism; Machiavellianism
(31).

<u>**Inclusive of other disorders:**</u>

<u>**Historical Clinical and Risk Management Scale-20 (HCR-20):**</u>

-measures: the risk of violence; violence; other antisocial behaviors; relationships; employment; substance use; major mental disorder; personality disorder; traumatic experiences; violent attitudes; treatment or supervision response; insight; violent ideation or intent; symptoms of major mental disorder; instability; risk management; professional services and plans; living situation; personal support; stress or coping;

-20 or more languages;

-Newest version: HCR-20 Version 3
(32).

Reasons for negative impacts on patients, in relation to <u>dysfunctional</u> (to nil) <u>empathy and remorsefulness</u> in rejectable and repellent healthcare professionals, include:

<u>Ethical boundaries</u>, to which the remorseless and/or unempathic healthcare worker does not adhere, incorporates, for instance:

-missed (ethical boundaries)

-misunderstood (ethics, and boundaries)

-reduced to nothing (ethics, and boundaries)

-acrimonious refusal of (ethics, and boundaries)

-supplanted for aggregated results (ethics)

-dehumanisation (versus ethics)

-antithetic and apathetic reasoning (about ethics)

-approbated misgivings (ethics, and boundaries)

-askewed priorities (away from ethics)

-sanctimonious underpinnings (regarding use of ethics)

-the (unstated, but often still recurrent) great divide between patient and caregiver.

Acrimoniousness toward patients for a myriad of reasons.

Inability, or refusal, to listen to patients, carers, other caregivers.

Along with the <u>obvious</u> physiological impacts of:

-when one is not listened to,

-related with,

-or has a treater with the incapacity to regret (and further) their
diagnostic and treatment based actions,

the <u>patient</u> is at <u>high risk</u> of medical error, serious medical error, multiple
critical incidents, never events,and so on.

In summary, a <u>complete compromisation</u> of patient safety, and quality of care, which
can lead inevitably to increased morbidity and higher risk of mortality.

Psychologically, and emotionally, the <u>impact</u> of lack of empathy and
remorselessness, knows even further no bounds.

Often impacting for a <u>life-time</u>, the patient is unnecessarily at the perceived <u>mercy</u> of
such doctors, nurses, and multiple other healthcare professionals.

For once misunderstood, or portrayed as something other than truthful, is to be:

-betrayed,

-put at risk,

-deceived, and

-their case covered-up,

thence comes a painful, ongoing journey of regret for ever trusting, confiding in, and seeking of (in any way) treatment-based empathic connection.

The patient, at the hands of an <u>anti-social, or narcissistic, treater</u> is at risk. That is obvious.

With all their nightmares rolled into one, the patient faces a <u>monstrous</u> situation, person, and task ahead of them.

For, <u>pleading</u> with the treater for empathy, or even basic humanity, is often well beyond their reach.

That is, <u>to be dead inside is always dead inside, to hate is always to hate, and to dehumanise occurs ad infinitem. Knocking on concrete, absolute.</u>

So too, the concomitant twisting of, and reliance on, some <u>extraneous clauses and rules,</u> which the treater believes will protect them from (sometimes) pending reports of professional misconduct, negligence, and law suits.

1/ Please define 'remorse'.

2/ What is 'usually an emotion elicited because others are aware..'?

3/ What is the difference between 'regret' and 'remorse'?

4/ Name 3 possible physiological effects of shame and guilt.

5/ Describe 'anticipated regret'.

6/ What are some of the rudimentary (non-regret based) reasons for 'open disclosure'?

7/ Summarise the typical process of open disclosure.

8/ What is involved in the third part of an 'open disclosure'/healthcare based apology?

9/ Describe the typical sequential stages of guilt.

10/ What is your understanding of 'empathy'?

11/ Does vicarious experience play a part in empathy?
     If so, how?

12/ What are the 2 primary types of empathy?

13/ Detail the difference between the 2 types of empathy.

14/ Provide 6 examples of remorselessness specific to healthcare
     environments.

15/ What is the forerunner of 'lack of remorse' within anti-social
     personality disorder?

16/ Define some burnout symptoms.

17/ Have you experienced, or witnessed, lack of empathy related to healthcare professional burnout?

18/ Provide 2 possible reasons for empathy deficits when trauma triggers are present.

19/ Define 'dissociative tendencies'.

20/ What is your understanding of 'emotional dysregulation'? How does it dovetail with lack of empathy?

21/ Which personality disorder is typically associated with negative effects upon affective empathy?

22/ Detail 4 specific factors of anti-social personality disorder.

23/ Provide 5 elements of narcissistic personality disorder.

24/ How is 'callousness' defined?

25/ Is callousness related to both narcissistic personality disorder and anti-social personality disorder? Please specify.

26/ Which disorder/s is/are associated with 'attention-seeking'?

27/ How could one define 'disinhibition'?

28/ Which factors are involved in disinhibition?

29/ Name 3 general assessment measures of empathy.

30/ Provide 1 example of a healthcare based empathy measure.

31/ Detail 1 empathy based assessment for patient use.

32/ What are the FFNI domains?

33/ What does the PCL-SV measure?

34/ Name an assessment measure which can be useful for both narcissistic personality disorder and anti-social personality disorder.

35/ How may one assess 'violent ideation or intent'?

36/ What is your understanding of ethical boundaries?

37/ Provide 5 examples of compromised ethical boundaries relevant to the remorseless and/or unempathic healthcare worker.

38/ What, in your opinion, are some of the reasons for acrimoniousness toward patients?

39/ Describe the types of risks to patients when a treater has incapacity for regret.

40/ What can happen as a result of a patient's perception of 'being at the mercy' of a remorseless and/or unempathic healthcare professional?

41/ Likewise (with question 40), with a healthcare treater who presents with anti-social or narcissistic traits?

APQ: Anti-Social Personality Questionnaire

CAPP SRS-CI: CAPP Semi-Structured- Clinical Interview

CAPP: Comprehensive Assessment of Psychopathic Personality

CARE: Consultation and Relational Empathy

DRS: Decision Regret Scale

DTDD: Dark Triad Dirty Dozen

ECRS: Empathy Construct Rating Scale

EETS: Emotional Empathic Tendency Scale

eg: example

EQ: Emotional Quotient

etc: etcetera

FFNI: Five Factor Narcissism Inventory

GPs: General Practitioners

HCR-20: Historical Clinical and Risk management scale- 20

IRI: Interpersonal Reactivity Index

JSE: Jefferson Scale of Physician Empathy

MASC: Movie for the Assessment of Social Cognition

MDEES: Multi-Dimensional Emotional Empathy Scale

MET: Multi-faceted Empathy Test

NPI: Narcissistic Personality Inventory

PCL-R: Psychopathy Checklist- Revised

PCL-SV: Psychopathy Checklist- Screening Version

PNI: Pathological Narcissism Inventory

PPI-R: Psychopathic Personality Inventory Revised

QCAE: Questionnaire of Cognitive and Affective Empathy

TES: Therapist Empathy Scale

REFERENCES

(1) Merriam-Webster, (2022), Remorse definition and meaning, www.merriam-webster.com

(2) The Brittanica Dictionary, (2022), Remorse, www.britannica.com

(3) APA dictionary: American Psychological Association, (2022), Remorse, www.dictionary.apa.org

(4) Lazare, A., Apology in medical practice: An emerging clinical skill, JAMA, Sept 20, 2006- Vol 296 (11), pp. 1400-1404.

(5) Merriam-Webster, (2022), Empathy definition and meaning, www.merriam-webster.com

(6) Cambridge dictionary, meaning of empathy, www.dictionary.cambridge.org

(7) APA dictionary: American Psychological Association, (2022), Émpathy, www.dictionary.apa.org

(8) American Psychiatric Association (2022), Diagnostic and Statistical Manual of Mental Disorders, 5th ed Text Revision: DSM-5-TR. Washington, D.C.: American Psychiatric Association Publishing, p. 884.

(9) Tophus, M.D. (2022), Burnout in Healthcare, Germany: Hilphma Publications.

(10) American Psychiatric Association (2022), Diagnostic and Statistical Manual of Mental Disorders, 5th ed Text Revision: DSM-5-TR. Washington, D.C.: American Psychiatric Association Publishing, p. 900.

(11) Foell, J., Brislin, S.J., Drislane, L.E., Dziobek, I. and Patrick, C.J., Creation and validation of an English-Language version of the Multifaceted Empathy Test (MET), Journal of Psychopathological Behavioral Assessment, 2018, 40, 431-439.

(12) Caruso, D.R. and Mayer, J.D. The Multidimensional Emotional Empathy Scale (MDEES), (1988), UNH Personality Lab 21.

(13) Dziobek, I., Fleck, S., Kalbe, E., Rogers, K., Hassenstab, J., Brand, M., Kessler, J., Wolke, J.K., Wolf, J.T., and Convit, A., Introducing MASC: A Movie for the Assessment of Social Cognition, Journal of Autism and Developmental Disorders, 2006, 36, 623-636.

(14) Davis, M.H., (1980), A multidimensional approach to individual differences in empathy, JSAS Catalog of Selected Documents in Psychology, 10: 85.

(15) Baron-Cohen, S. and Wheelwright, S.,The Empathy Quotient: An investigation of adults with Asperger Syndrome or high functioning autism, and normal sex differences, Journal of Autism and Developmental Disorders, 2004, 34, 163-175.

(16) La Monica, E.L., Construct validity of an empathy instrument. Research in Nursing and Health, 1981, 4, 389-400.

(17) Hojat, M., Mangione, S., Nasca, T.J., Cohen, M.J.M., Gonnella, J.S., Erdmann, J.B., Veloski, J. and Magee, M., The Jefferson Scale of Empathy: Development and preliminary psychometric data, Educational and Psychological Measurement, 2001, 61, 349-365.

(18) Decker, S.E., Nich, C., Carroll, K.M. and Martino, S., Development of the Therapist Empathy Scale, Behav Cogn Psychother, 2014 May, 42(3), 339-354.

(19) Reniers, R.L., Corcoran, R., Drake, R., Shryane, N.M. and Völlm, B.A., The QCAE: a Questionnaire of Cognitive and Affective Empathy, J Pers Assess, 2011 Jan, 93(1), 84-95.

(20) Mehrabian, A. and Epstein, N., A measure of emotional empathy, Journal of Personality, 1972, 40, 525-543.

(21) Brehaut, J.C., O'Connor, A.M., Wood, T.J., Hack, T.F., Siminoff, L., Gordon, E. & Feldman-Stewart, D., Validation of a decision regret scale, Medical Decision Making 2003; 23 (4): 281-92.

(22) Mercer, S.W., Watt, G.C.M., Maxwell, M. and Heaney, D.H., The development and preliminary validation of the Consultation and Relational Empathy (CARE) measure: an empathy-based consultation process measure, Family Practice, 2004, 21(3), 699-705.

(23) Glover, N., Miller, J.D., Lynam, D.R., Crego, C. and Widiger, T.A.,The Five-Factor Narcissism Inventory: A Five-Factor measure of narcissistic personality traits, Journal of Personality Assessment, 2012, Vol.94 (5): 500-512.

(24) Raskin, R.N. and Hall, C.S. (1979), A Narcissistic Personality Inventory, Psychological Reports, 45, 590-590.

(25) Pincus, A.L., Ansell, E.B., Pimentel, C.A., Cain, N.M., Wright, A.G.C. and Levy, K.N., Initial construction and validation of the pathological narcissism inventory, Psychological Assessment, Sept 2009, 21(3): 365-379.

(26) Hare, R.D., Harpur, T.J., Hakstian, A.R., Forth, A.E. and Hart, S.D., The Revised Psychopathy Checklist: Reliability and factor structure, Psychological Assessment, 1990, 2(3), 338-341.

(27) Hart, S.D., Cox, D.N. and Hare, R.D. (1996), Manual for the Screening Version of Psychopathy Checklist Revised (PCL:SV), Toronto: Multi-Health Systems.

(28) Lilienfeld, S.O. and Widows, M.R. (2005), Psychopathic Personality Inventory-Revised (PPI-R): Professional Manual, Lutz, FL: Psychological Assessment Resources.

(29) Cooke, D.J., Hart, S.D., Logan, C., and Michie, C., Explicating the construct of psychopathy: Development and validation of a conceptual model, the Comprehensive Assessment of Psychopathic Personality (CAPP), International Journal of Forensic Mental Health, 2012, 11, 4, 242-252.

(30) Blackburn, R. & Fawcett, D., The Antisocial Personality Questionnaire: An inventory for assessing personality deviation in offender populations..., European Journal of Psychological Assessment, 2006, Vol 15(1), 14-24.

(31) Jonason, P.K. and Webster, G., The Dirty Dozen: A concise measure of the dark triad, Psychological Assessment, 2010, 22(2), 4220-432.

(32) Douglas, K.S., Hart, S.D., Webster, C.D., Belfrage, H., Guy, L.S. and Wilson, C.M., Historical-Clinical-Risk Management-20, Version 3 (HCR-20 V3): Development and overview, International Journal of Forensic Mental Health, 2014, Vol 13, Issue 2.

ability 16+

acceptance 30

acceptation 13

accomplishment 18

accountability 16

acrimonious 37

acrimoniousness 44

action/s 10; 11; 14; 16; 17; 24; 38

ad infinitem 39

admission 16

adolescence 34

adulthood 23; 34

adverse healthcare event 12

affective 26; 29

affective- empathic processing 19

affective empathy 14; 21; 28; 42

aggregated 37

aggression 22; 35

anger 13; 20

angst 8

anguish 10

another's shoes 15

antagonism 24; 25; 32

anticipated regret 11; 40

antisocial 35; 36

anti-social 25+

anti-social behavior 33

anti-social behaviors 22; 34

antithetic 37

anxiety 17

apathetic 37

apologies 12; 13

apology 13; 40

apparatus 8

approbated 37

APQ 35; 46

arrogance 12; 29

arrogant 23

askewed 37

at risk 39

attention 27

attention-seeker 23

attention-seeking 25; 43

attitudes 36

attitudinal 30

attuned 30

attunement 30

avoidance 10; 11; 19; 20; 35

avoidant 21

aware 10; 14; 19; 40

awry 11

bad 10

behavioral reaction 10

behavioral traits 8

betrayed 39

borderline 21

burnout 18; 41; 42

callous 23

callous disregard 16; 21

CAPP 35

CAPP SRS 35

CAPP SRS-CI 46

capture 30

CARE 31+

caregiver 37

caregivers 38

case 11; 39

clauses 39

client 29+

client- settings 29

client's inner world 30

clinical decision-making 16; 17

clinical neutrality 29

cognitive 30

cognitive- empathic processing 19

cognitive empathy 15; 21

cognitive- empathy 27

cognitive framework 30

coldness 16

colleagues 8; 16

communicate 20

communicated 14

communication 12; 29

compassion 29

compassionate 14

comprehend 27

compromisation 38

compromization 21

computerized 27

concentration 19

concepts 8

conceptualises 23

concern 17; 22; 24; 28; 30

conduct 10

confiding 39

conflict 20

connection 20; 39

conscientiousness 32

consequences 10; 26

consideration 26

contact 29; 31

contemplation 10

contempt 16

context 19

contexts 34

coping 20; 36

covered-up 39

criminal offending 34

critical incident 12; 16

critical incidents 38

crying 27

dead 39

deceit 16

deceitful 23

deceitfulness 24; 34

deceived 38

deficiency 34

deficits 19; 22; 42

dehumanisation 37

dehumanise 39

delay 19

deleterious 16

depersonalization 18

description 12; 21; 22

detached 19

devaluing 33

deviance 35

diagnosed 23

diagnosis 22

diagnostic 21; 37

Dirty Dozen Test 36; 46

dispositional 28

dispositions 35

dissociative 19; 42

distractibility 26

distress 19; 31

doctors 38

dominance 34

dotting the i's 12

DRS 31; 46

DTDD 36; 46

dysfunctional 37

ECRS 29; 46

EETS 31; 46

effects 24+

emotional 10+

emotional contagion 27; 31

emotional detachment 33

emotional dysregulation 20; 42

emotional- empathy 14; 27

emotional exhaustion 18

emotionally 38

emotions 10; 14; 15; 18; 19; 27

empathic processing 18; 19

employment 36

endangering 8

entitlement 23; 33

envious 23

EQ 28

ethical boundaries 37; 44

ethical dilemmas 8

exhaustion 11

experiences 14; 30; 31; 36

experiencing 14; 16

explicit 14

exploitativeness 33

exploits 23

express 18

expression 12; 13; 14

expressiveness 30

extraneous 39

extraversion 32; 35

factual 12

fantasising 23

fantasy 28; 33

fearless 34

feedback 31

feel 14; 18; 27

feeling/s 10+

FFNI 32; 43; 47

fightability 20

flashbacks 19

forbearance 13

forgivable 18

frame of reference 14

frightening 8

frustrated 20

future 10; 13; 16; 26

glibness 16; 20

GPs 31; 47

grandiose 23; 32; 33

grandiosity 24; 33

gratification 26

great divide 37

guilt 10; 11; 13; 16; 24; 40; 41

harm 16

harmful 24

hate 39

hated 8

HCR-20 36; 47

head will explode 18

health professional students 29

healthcare 8; 11; 12; 13; 16; 21; 29; 31; 37; 38; 40; 42; 43; 44; 45

healthcare environment 8; 20

healthcare environments 12; 29

healthcare field 8

healthcare incident 12

healthcare professional 21; 42

healthcare professionals 29; 38

hiding 33

historical 19; 22; 36; 47

history 34

hostility 25

human resources 12

humanity 39

humility 13

humour 29

hurting 17

hypervigilance 19

ideation 36; 44

imagining 14

imminent 11

impact 16; 38

impacts 8; 37; 38

impulse control 20

impulsive 22; 26; 34

impulsivity 26; 34

inability 18; 38

inaction 11

incites 8

increased 38

indicator 22

inevitably 38

inner experience 30

insight 36

insomnia 11

insouciance 16

instability 36

intent 36; 44

intentions 28

internal disclosure 16

interpersonal 23; 28; 35; 47

intolerance 20

intrapersonal 35

IRI 28; 47

irresponsibility 22; 26

irresponsible 34

irritability 19

items 27; 28; 29; 30; 31; 32; 33; 34; 35; 36

job duties 20

job role 20

journey 39

JSE 29; 47

justifications 16

languages 36

law suits 39

Lazare 13

learning 26

life philosophy 8

life-time 38

listened 38

listening 20

living 36

longevity 35

lying 22

Machiavellianism 36

malignant narcissism 24

manage 12

management 12

mandatory obligation 12

manipulative 22; 23

manipulativeness 24

MASC 28; 47

MDEES 27; 47

medical error 8; 12; 16; 38

medical event 17

medical students 29

memories 12

memory dysfunction 19

memory recall 19

mental disorder 36

mercy 38; 44

MET 27; 47

misgivings 37

missed 37

mistreating 17

misunderstood 37; 39

monstrous 39

morbidity 38

mortality 38

movie 28; 47

narcissistic 32

narcissistic traits 32; 45

needs 17; 20

negative 10; 17; 24; 27; 31; 37; 42

negative action 11

negative emotions 10; 19

negligence 39

negotiation 13

neuroticism 32

never events 8; 38

nightmares 11; 39

no bounds 38

non-diagnostic 32

non-forensic 34

non-trauma 20

nothing 37

NPI 32; 47

nurses 29; 38

nursing students 29

objectively 14

observation 30; 35

obsessive-compulsive 21

occurred 12

online simulation 30

open disclosure 12; 13; 40

openness 32

opinions 8

opposition 8

overwhelmed 18

overwhelms 19

pack mentality 16

painful 39

parameters 21

paranoid 35

past 10; 11; 14; 26

patient 39

patient- centered 31

patient empathy 31

patient feedback 12

patient safety 38

patient- settings 29

patient/s 20+

PCL-R 33; 48

PCL-SV 33; 43; 48

perception 19; 44

perceptions 14; 28

performance appraisers 9

peripheral 30

personal 18; 19

personal distress 28

personal growth 29

personal support 36

personality disorders 21

perspective 17; 28; 30

phenomenological 16

physical 11

physicians 29

physiological 11; 16; 38; 40

pictures 27

plans 12; 36

pleading 39

plight 19

PNI 33; 48

portrayed 39

positive 27; 31

post-adverse event 9

power 23

PPI-R 34; 48

practised 20

pragmatic 20

presence 19

present 14; 19; 42; 45

preventative 11

prevention 12

priorities 37

problems 24

processing 13; 18; 19

professional misconduct 39

professional services 36

propensity 20

protect 39

proximal 30

psychological 19

psychologically 38

psychopathy 21; 25; 33; 34; 35; 36; 48

punishment 10

pursues 8

QCAE 30; 48

quality of care 31; 38

questions 28

rage 33; 35

rationalization 16

reactivity 20; 28; 47

reasoning 37

reasons 18; 37; 38; 40; 42; 44

reciprocal 19

recognize 27

recruiters 9

reduced 18; 37

refusal 16; 20; 37; 38

regret 10; 11; 12; 16; 38; 39; 40; 44

rejection 8; 20; 22

relate 10; 19

related 19; 20; 38; 42; 43

relating 20

relationships 36

reliance 39

remedied 10

reports 39

reprimands 8

repudiation 13

resentment 20; 35

resonate 30

resourcefulness 8

respond 14

respondent 34

response 31; 36

responsive 27

responsiveness 30; 31

responsivity 30

results 37

right & wrong 8

rigid perfectionism 26

risk 11; 36; 39

risk management 36

risk taking 26

risk-taker 22

risk-taking 16

rules 39

rumination 11

sadness 11; 13

sanctimonious 37

scales 35

schizotypal 21

screens 33

seeking 39

self 10; 23; 33

self-centered 34

self-control 35

self-enhancement 33

self-esteem 33; 35

self-focus 18

self-focussed 16

self-protection 29

self-protective 20

self-reproach 10

self-sacrificing 33

sensitive 14

sensitivity 20

sequential 13; 41

settings 29; 31; 35

severity 33; 35

shame 10; 11; 13; 40

shamelessness 13

sharing 27

shock 13

situation 13; 14; 16; 17; 36; 39

social norms 22

sociopathy 21; 32

sorry 10; 12

special 23

special others 23

stages 13; 41

state 19

stimuli 26

stress 36

subclinical 32

subscales 28; 32

substance use 36

success 20

successor 8

suffering 17; 27

superiority 16

supervision 36

supplanted 37

suspicion 35

sympathy 29; 31

symptom 23

symptomatology 11; 21

symptoms 18; 33; 35; 36; 41

task 11; 39

tendencies 19; 42

TES 30; 48

test 27

thoughts 14; 26; 28

tolerance 29

trauma triggers 18; 19

traumatic 32

traumatic event 18

treater 38; 39; 44; 45

treatment 31; 36; 38; 39

triggers 12

trust 29

trusting 39

truthful 39

twisting 39

underpinnings 37

understand 14; 15

understanding 14; 19; 30; 41; 42; 44

unnecessarily 38

unthinking 16

unwillingness 13

version 28

vicariously 14

vindictiveness 20

violence 36

violent 36; 44

vulnerability 19; 33

vulnerable 19; 32

warmth 30

willingness 13; 31

work activities 18

wrong 10